EXTREME SPORTS AND STUNTS™

EXTREME PARKOUR

Monique Vescia

rosen publishing's rosen central®

New York

Published in 2020 by The Rosen Publishing Group, Inc.
29 East 21st Street, New York, NY 10010

First Edition

Library of Congress Cataloging-in-Publication Data

Names: Vescia, Monique, author.
Title: Extreme parkour / Monique Vescia.
Description: First Edition. | New York : Rosen Publishing, 2020. | Series: Extreme Sports and Stunts | Audience: Grade level for this book is grades 5–8. | Includes bibliographical references and index.
Identifiers: LCCN 2019008621| ISBN 9781725347434 (library bound) | ISBN 9781725347427 (paperback)
Subjects: LCSH: Parkour—Juvenile literature. | Obstacle racing—Training—Juvenile literature. | Extreme sports—Juvenile literature.
Classification: LCC GV1068 .V47 2020 | DDC 796.42/5—dc23
LC record available at https://lccn.loc.gov/2019008621

Manufactured in the United States of America

Disclaimer: Do not attempt this sport without wearing proper safety gear and taking safety precautions.

CONTENTS

INTRODUCTION

As the twenty-first century began, moviegoers marveled at the sight of action heroes moving at breakneck speed through cityscapes, scaling walls, and vaulting over barriers. These acrobatic and death-defying movements belonged to a new physical disciple called parkour (pronounced par-KOOR). It was based on the French term for a military-style obstacle course, *parcours du combattant*, meaning "obstacle course." Practitioners of this art of movement, known as *traceurs* (tray-SURZ), treat the urban environment like the giant obstacle course that the name suggests, which they navigate with incredible speed, skill, and grace. Videos of fantastic feats went viral on YouTube, attracting new audiences and practitioners around the world. Before long, parkour began appearing in music videos and on television shows.

As parkour's popularity grew, so did debates about how to categorize it. Many insisted that parkour was not a sport. They called it a movement art and stressed that in parkour, mental discipline was as important as physical training. Arguments raged between parkour purists and those who saw the practice in a different light. Parkour eventually gave rise to freerunning, a more acrobatic and artistic version of parkour. Soon, other variations of it appeared.

Parkour is a low-cost activity—one reason for its increasing popularity. It requires no special equipment and can be practiced by individuals of any age in good physical condition. Parkour gyms have opened,

A skilled athlete makes use of the features of the urban landscape. Safety gear isn't always used in parkour, so the sport should only be practiced by experienced professionals or in a parkour gym.

but many athletes begin their training with groups of friends in city streets and parks.

While parkour is available to everyone, only the most dedicated athletes, like Jesse la Flair and Katie McDonnell, become true artists of this discipline. Their heart-stopping moves have made parkour among the most popular sports viewed online, with many millions of views. So let's leap into the world of extreme parkour!

CHAPTER ONE

THE ART OF MOVEMENT

Many sports, such as wrestling and discus throwing, date back to ancient Greece, and the first Olympic games in 776 BCE. In contrast, parkour is a very new athletic activity, dating from the 1990s. But the seeds that would grow into parkour were planted more than a century earlier. And it all started with a volcanic explosion.

GEORGES HÉBERT AND THE NATURAL METHOD

In 1902, a volcano on the Caribbean island of Martinique erupted, instantly killing more than twenty-eight thousand people. A French naval officer stationed there named Georges Hébert helped evacuate the survivors. He saw that people native to the island navigated the obstacles along the evacuation route with more grace and skill than the Europeans being rescued.

Back in France, Hébert developed a regimen of physical training based on what he witnessed in Martinique, which he called the Natural Method. He considered it essential to total body fitness. The training included swimming, climbing, running, and navigating an outdoor obstacle course. Hébert combined this physical workout with an emphasis on mental and emotional development. Hébert's Natural Method, which drew on the theories of other physical educators, influenced the training of French soldiers during the Vietnam War (1955–1975). One of these soldiers was a young man named Raymond Belle.

STRONGER BY LEAPS AND BOUNDS

Born in Vietnam in 1939, Raymond Belle was separated from his parents during the First Indochina War (1946–1954). The French military took him in at the age of seven, and he was raised at the Da Lat military orphanage. The frequent abuse that young Raymond suffered in this setting drove him to improve his strength and physical fitness to better protect himself. He would sneak out at night and train silently. At the orphanage, Raymond also had military training, which included regular workouts on an obstacle course.

When he was nineteen, Belle moved to France and joined the *sapeurs-pompiers*, the military branch of firefighters. To keep his body at the peak of physical fitness, Belle devised a workout based on Hébert's program. He became a legend in the *sapeurs-*

Georges Hébert, shown here, seated, developed an influential physical fitness program, from which Belle created his own regimen.

pompiers for his abilities. He could scale a burning building without a ladder, scampering up a drainpipe and along window ledges.

DAVID BELLE AND THE "ART OF DISPLACEMENT"

Born in Fécamp, France, in 1973, David Belle, son of Raymond Belle, inherited his father's obsession with physical fitness. He participated in gymnastics and track and field and always wanted to be outdoors in the forests of that region. David loved to test himself by moving over and around obstacles without slowing down, and he developed extraordinary athletic skills, strength, balance, and stamina.

When David was fifteen, his family moved to Lisses (pronounced LEASE), a suburb about 35 miles (56 kilometers) from Paris. He soon adapted his techniques to this new urban environment, scaling concrete walls and jumping off rooftops with grace and precision. In Lisses, David met Sébastien Foucan and other young men who were eager to practice his methods for mastering obstacles. They challenged one another to climb higher and jump farther, to improve balance and mental focus. What started as a form of play soon became a serious undertaking.

David's brother Jeff filmed David practicing what he called the art of displacement, moving with speed, grace, and efficiency from one place to another. He showed the video to a French television station, and soon David and his friends began attracting media attention. You can see these early videos of David Belle on YouTube.

In 1997, David and eight other top athletes of this art of displacement formed a group called Yamakasi. The name may sound Japanese, but it is a word of the an African Lingala language meaning "strong man, strong spirit." The Yamakasi ideal was to become strong, not just physically, but also mentally and ethically. The group inspired a 2001 film called *Yamakasi,* in which a group of daredevils scale tall buildings and steal money for a boy's heart transplant. Many of the founding members of Yamakasi starred in the film.

The term "Yamakasi" now signifies a traditional style of training that precedes the split between parkour and freerunning.

Eventually, David Belle and Sébastien Foucan came to disagree about the nature of their art form. Belle began using the term *parkour* to describe the method of training he had developed. For Belle, parkour was a discipline of self-improvement, a method of testing the mind and spirit by challenging the body. Practitioners of parkour moved quickly and efficiently to overcome a series of

PARKOUR MANIA

Dan Iaboni, owner of the Monkey Vault parkour gym in Toronto, Canada, began teaching himself parkour after seeing an online video.

Parkour has influenced all forms of visual media, including television, advertising, music videos, and video games. Many high-grossing action films have introduced audiences to mind-blowing parkour moves. Characters leap the gaps between skyscrapers and launch themselves from the roofs of moving cars—two things you should never try. Elite parkour athletes such as Sébastien Foucan and Jesse La Flair have been hired to do stunts in action films. You can see some examples of parkour and freerunning in films such as *Prince of Persia: The Sands of Time* (2010), *Assassin's Creed* (2016), *Brick Mansions* (2014), and *Tracers* (2015).

Parkour fever infected the United States and Russia and soon became a worldwide phenomenon. The singer Madonna included parkour scenes in her music videos for "Hung Up" (2005) and "Jump" (2006). *MTV's Ultimate Parkour Challenge*, set in Southern California, aired between 2009 and 2010. This TV miniseries helped introduce parkour to a mainstream American audience. Gyms dedicated to parkour began opening in cities around the United States. By 2019, the United Kingdom–based parkour team STORROR's YouTube channel had racked up twenty to forty million views each month.

obstacles, pushing their own limits. They weren't interested in impressing onlookers with flashy moves. Foucan, on the other hand, wanted to incorporate more acrobatics and self-expression into the training.

Foucan eventually split off from the original group because he wanted to pursue a style of parkour more focused on creative expression, which came to be known as freerunning. Freerunning combines traditional parkour movements with gymnastics and acrobatics and has become associated with fancy flips and other dazzling stunts that show off the creativity of the individual practitioner. German-born freerunner Jason Paul and Team Farang have become world famous practicing this style of parkour.

PARKOUR FEVER

Before long, interest in both parkour and freerunning spread from France to the rest of Europe. The United Kingdom became one of the first places to embrace this art of movement. In 2003, Sébastien Foucan and other French freerunners starred in a documentary called *Jump London.* A sequel, *Jump Britain* (2005), came two years later.

IS PARKOUR A SPORT?

People disagree about whether or not parkour should be called a sport. Parkour has no rules, no referees, and no point system. The original Yamakasi group did not consider parkour a competitive activity. They believed the spirit of parkour was at odds with the competitive nature of team sports and that parkour should be free from commercialization. But the parkour genie was out of the bottle, so to speak, and before long, worldwide interest in the activity led to the first planned events and competitions.

In 2009, the organization American Parkour (APK) asked the parkour community to define the practice of parkour and its purpose. According to APK, parkour training should focus on safety, personal responsibility, and self-improvement. Parkour practitioners should strive for a long life, keeping fit, and flexible as they age. APK discourages reckless stunts that may endanger people and property. The group agreed on the following values: community, humility, positive collaboration, sharing of knowledge, the importance of play in human life, and respect for all people, places, and spaces.

In 2017, the Fédération Internationale de Gymnastique (FIG) began trying to label parkour as a gymnastic activity. Members of the parkour community fiercely opposed this action, sharing the hashtag #WeAreNOTGymnastics on Twitter.

The following year, four representatives of the FIG parkour commission resigned in protest. In an open letter, they complained that the international parkour community was being kept in the dark. The representatives warned that, "We see problems that [worry] us for the future of parkour." In spite of this ongoing battle, FIG has staged Parkour World Cups since 2017.

That year, the United Kingdom became the first country to officially recognize parkour as a sport. This classification meant that organizations teaching parkour could apply for government funds. This opened the way for parkour to be practiced in schools.

IS PARKOUR LEGAL?

Governments often pass laws to address a problem. Typically, decisions about whether to outlaw activities such as parkour are up to individual towns, cities, and states. Because parkour is a new activity, some lawmakers may be unfamiliar with it. Irresponsible traceurs damaging public property or endangering their own or others' lives could lead to the passing of laws prohibiting parkour. This type of disrespectful behavior hurts the parkour community as a whole. Traceurs should act as representatives of parkour, spreading the word about its benefits, and attracting more enthusiasts and supporters to this exciting art of movement.

THE FUTURE OF PARKOUR

At the time of this writing, parkour has no official governing body, which means it cannot be part of the Olympic Games. This lack of organization has made it hard for parkour to define itself. The United Kingdom–based Parkour Earth and a US organization called the International Parkour Federation have competed for the right to fight against the FIG takeover.

So what's next for this art of movement? Will parkour be taken over by gymnastics, or will it win its fight for independence? Will traceurs begin displaying product logos on their gear like cyclists and basketball players do? Stay tuned!

CHAPTER TWO

OBSTACLES AS OPPORTUNITIES

Anyone in relatively good physical shape can learn parkour. This natural method of physical training can be practiced in an urban or rural environment, in a designated parkour park, or in a school gym. No expensive apparatus or gear is required—just a decent pair of shoes. The only equipment necessary is the human body and a variety of obstacles.

"Parkour vision" lets the athlete see urban features as the challenging components of a giant obstacle course.

AN URBAN ART OF MOVEMENT

Have you ever sprawled on your back and imagined yourself walking around the ceiling as if it's a floor? People who learn parkour say that a funny thing happens after they've been doing it for a while. They begin to see their environment in a radically different light, a phenomenon some call parkour vision. As Dan Edwardes writes in *The Parkour and Freerunning Handbook*, "Very swiftly you find yourself seeing city streets, squares, stairways, even simple sidewalks as something quite different. Everywhere becomes an opportunity for movement." The parkour practitioner no longer feels limited by his or her physical environment when the city becomes a space for play and freedom.

GYMS AND PARKS FOR PARKOUR

As interest in parkour spread from France to other countries in Europe and eventually to the United States, some people started opening gyms where parkour could be taught and practiced. Though some argue that the artificial environment of a gym goes against the original spirit of parkour, these gyms have proven to be very popular.

BEHAVE YOURSELF!

An important principle of parkour is respect for one's environment. Responsible parkour athletes take care not to damage property, whether natural (a tree) or manmade (a piece of public art), when practicing their moves. Traceurs who post videos of themselves trespassing in restricted areas and vaulting over fragile historical structures give parkour a bad name and risk endangering themselves in the process. These actions may prompt local authorities to pass laws banning parkour in a particular city or town. Such restrictions will end up negatively impacting others in the parkour community.

Most major cities in the United States now have at least one parkour gym, and many have several. Parkour gyms are designed to safely teach students the skills of rolling, running, vaulting, climbing, and jumping. By mastering these techniques, students learn to move through an obstacle course as efficiently as possible. Obstacles may include a combination of warped walls, climbing bars, foam pits, large pillars, and boxes, many of which can be rearranged. Regular fitness routines can become boring if you repeat the same series of exercises at each workout. Parkour training emphasizes finding creative solutions to overcoming obstacles and other physical challenges.

Parkour lessons in a gym can be expensive and therefore are not accessible to everyone. Many prefer

Designated spaces where traceurs can practice their moves, like this parkour park in the eastern European nation of Belarus, honor the outdoor origins of this sport.

to practice their moves outdoors, on college campuses, playgrounds, beaches, athletic fields, and in forests. Cities have begun building outdoor parkour parks where traceurs can jam, or gather to practice their art. Dallas, Texas; Boise, Idaho; and San Francisco and Lathrop, California, are just

PARKOUR GEAR: COME AS YOU ARE

Traceurs wear comfortable clothing that allows for maximum freedom of movement. T-shirts are fine, as long as they fit comfortably. If too tight, the athlete will feel constrained, and the fabric may tear, whereas an oversized shirt may snag on something. A long-sleeved tee helps protect the elbows from scrapes. Since hands and arms take a beating during parkour training, some people wear gloves to protect their palms. When they are mastering a difficult movement, some traceurs wear elbow pads, though protective gear is rarely worn in competition since it restricts movement.

The rules for shirts also apply to pants: not too tight and not too loose. Jeans are out because denim doesn't necessarily move with the body and may be overly baggy. Some traceurs wear shorts, while others prefer sweatpants or track pants, which help protect the lower legs from scrapes and cuts. Some parkour enthusiasts wear a beanie to keep their hair out of their eyes.

Shoes are the most important element of a practitioner's gear. Most parkour athletes don't invest in expensive footwear because it wears out quickly. Shoes should be comfortable, supportive, and fit snugly on the foot. Some people prefer shoes with thin soles so they can feel the different surfaces beneath their feet. Others wear "five-finger" shoes with an individual space for each toe.

The sign of a serious traceur is not what he wears but how much control the traceur has over that remarkable machine, the human body.

some cities with outdoor spaces designed specifically for parkour.

GETTING SCHOOLED

In 2017, the American Parkour Academy (APK) teamed up with physical education (PE) departments to bring parkour to public schools in Washington, D.C., and Maryland. Originally targeted to twenty-seven schools, the program proved so successful that it was expanded to forty schools, with plans to add charter schools and after-school programs as well.

Parkour helps kids learn movement skills and body control while building self-confidence. Mark Toorock, founder of APK, said in a press release, "For kids still learning fundamentals of how their bodies work, it is like practicing the alphabet by singing the song rather than memorizing the letters." As they master basic skills of balance, jumping and landing, vaulting, and crawling, kids move on to more difficult challenges. Parkour has its origins in play, and the students in this program have a great time learning the basic moves in a safe environment.

Elementary, middle, and high schools in the Chicago area have also partnered with a local parkour organization to teach students this movement art. Incorporating parkour training into a traditional PE curriculum does not necessarily require any added expense. Gym mats, gymnastic apparatus, and other typical PE equipment can be used for teaching parkour skills. By teaming up with schools, parkour organizations spread the word about parkour and attract new members to local gyms.

CHAPTER THREE

MASTERING MOMENTUM

Parkour training is based on practicing natural human movements. Training conditions the body, gradually improving strength, flexibility, balance, agility, cardiovascular health, and coordination. The goal of the training is to become fully functional: capable of responding to every physical challenge in one's environment.

While an elite traceur may execute amazing moves with incredible skill, the components of every parkour routine are basic movements that almost anyone can learn to perform.

Successfully completing a parkour jump like this means mastering techniques for landing without injury.

THE CORE MOVEMENTS

The basic actions of running, climbing, and jumping form the building blocks for every parkour sequence. Traceurs work to master these and other movements and to execute them safely and efficiently.

All parkour sequences begin with running, an acceleration toward an obstacle, so training includes time spent on this skill, including light jogging, sprints, and distance running. Parkour also includes a wide variety of jumps, such as standing and running jumps, single- and double-leg jumps, drops, and vaults. These require leg strength to push off from the ground or from an obstacle. Finally, many movements in parkour incorporate climbing. This training improves grip and builds upper-body strength.

BALANCING, LANDING, AND ROLLING

Good balance is fundamental to parkour and underlies all other movements. Traceurs practice their balancing skills on two feet and on all fours, moving along surfaces of varying thicknesses and orientations (both flat and slanted). In a city or suburb, curbs and low railings provide opportunities to practice balance work.

When a person drops from a height and lands on a hard surface, it sends a shock through her or his body. Such an impact can cause long-term damage to the human skeleton, ligaments, and tendons. Learning how to land well and safely is essential to parkour training. A proper landing technique will absorb and redistribute the shock of impact, protecting the body from injury. Parkour practitioners master landing correctly from short distances before gradually moving on to larger drops.

Landing safely is essential to the practice of parkour and freerunning. According to Dan Edwardes, cofounder of Parkour Generations, these basic techniques can help insure a safe landing:

- Land quietly: Softer landings are easier on the body since the muscles, rather than bones and joints, absorb the impact.
- Align the body: Keeping the legs in the same position as each other distributes the impact of a landing equally throughout the body.
- Land on the balls of the feet: Landing on the front part of the foot, rather than flat-footed or on the heels, directs the impact into the muscles of the ankles and lower legs. It also gives the body better stability.
- Remain relaxed: Staying loose and bouncy instead of locking one's legs will let the body better absorb the impact of a landing.
- Exhale on the landing: Holding one's breath makes the body stiff, whereas breathing helps the body relax.

Rolls are another technique for redistributing the impact of a drop safely away from the body. Unlike a gymnast, who somersaults by tucking her head and

A well-executed roll helps protect the spine and distributes the shock of landing safely away from the traceur's body.

rolling along her spine, a traceuse (a female traceur) rolls diagonally on her back from one shoulder to the opposite hip. This puts muscle instead of bone in contact with the ground. Rolls must be executed immediately upon contact, otherwise the shock of impact will remain in the body. As with landing skills, it takes practice to master these techniques.

LACHE

In addition to the core movements of running, jumping, and climbing that make up a parkour sequence, if you watch traceurs practicing outside or in videos online, you will see other moves frequently incorporated into each sequence. Because parkour originated in France, many of these movements have French names.

PARKOUR MASH-UPS

Parkour may be a relative newcomer to the scene, but people have begun combining it with other more established sports, movement arts, and martial arts. Team Ryouko, a martial arts stunt team based in Toronto, Canada, brings together elements from capoeira (an Afro-Brazilian martial art combining dance, acrobatics, and music) and parkour. Other gyms teach a blend of parkour and Krav Maga, self-defense techniques first developed by the Israeli army. The famous theatrical production company Cirque du Soleil combines parkour moves with acrobatics in its artistic dance performances. And some dog trainers are even teaching canine parkour!

Some of these include swings and hanging movements (called *lache* [LASH]), which means "loose" in French, in which traceurs move across the underside of bars. These moves let a traceuse use her entire body to generate momentum.

SAUT DE CHAT

The *saut de chat* (SO-du-SHAH) or "cat leap" is also called the kong vault. To execute this move, a traceuse approaches an obstacle head-on. Planting her hands on top of the obstacle, she propels herself into a dive. At the same time, she tucks her legs, bringing them up under her chest and through her arms. Pushing off with her hands, she vaults over the obstacle.

TIC-TAC

The tic-tac is a stepping movement in which the traceur runs along a wall, pushing off on the balls of the feet to gain height. It is usually combined with other techniques, such as a cat leap or a precision landing. In a 360 tic-tac, the traceur executes a 360-degree spin while stepping along a vertical surface, generating even more momentum.

CAT-TO-CAT

Imagine a cat clinging to the wall in a crouching position, then pushing off hard and twisting in the air, to land clinging to the top of another obstacle behind or to the side. This move helps develop physical coordination in the air.

CLEARING

The French term for clearing is *franchissement* (frohn-shiz-MON), a category of movements that carry the traceur through, under, or around an obstacle. Clearing includes *underbars*, grasping a bar and propelling the body through a gap underneath.

A traceuse gleefully vaults over a guardrail. Part of the joy of "flow" is the sensation of a well-trained body responding with grace and agility to each new challenge.

GO WITH THE FLOW

After mastering the basic elements of parkour, it's time to put these movements together into a parkour sequence or route. The real beauty of parkour is when individual components become part of a continuous flow of movement from one obstacle to the next. Once an athlete has learned the techniques of parkour, he or she can combine them in a nearly limitless number of sequences to move swiftly and smoothly from one place to another—a true art of displacement. Ideally, each movement in the sequence should become as instinctual as walking or going down a flight of stairs.

CHAPTER FOUR

STAYING SAFE

In one episode of the television comedy series *The Office*, the characters shout "Parkour!" and clamber clumsily over furniture and their fellow coworkers, knocking over lamps and laptops. Outside, one jumps awkwardly from the roof of a truck into an empty cardboard refrigerator box. These funny scenes, and hundreds of "parkour fail" videos online, highlight a serious problem, however. If you are not properly trained, parkour can be dangerous.

The goal of parkour training is to condition the body to safely perform any number of physical maneuvers. As with any physical activity, however, attempting parkour without adequate training and safety precautions can result in

This airborne descent down the stairs looks effortless, but a misstep can do some serious damage when one doesn't take the proper safety precautions.

serious injury or even death. Videos of dazzling parkour routines on the internet have inspired some amateurs to try imitating these moves without the necessary training, with tragic results. After the release of the parkour film *Yamakasi* (2001), two deaths occurred because of copycat behavior.

A 2016 scientific report about parkour-related injuries gathered information from 1,700 respondents. The study showed that training outside or alone was riskier than practicing in a gym and in the company of others. Researchers discovered that landing was the most frequently reported cause of injury. According to this survey, the ankle, knee, and foot are the parts of the body that traceurs injure the most. Most parkour-related injuries are sprains and bruises and generally take less than two weeks to heal. Engaging in any physical activity carries risks, but many of the athletes sampled said that their parkour training actually helped them to avoid injuries while practicing this sport.

PRACTICE PARKOUR SAFETY

Serious parkour practitioners stress the importance of mastering the fundamentals of parkour before gradually attempting more advanced movements and techniques. Taking the time to warm up and down properly reduces the risk of injury. Smart traceurs learn how to land and roll properly before attempting more difficult moves. Traceurs need to know their own limitations and to recognize when they are becoming fatigued. Smart traceurs don't attempt a move until they feel confident they can execute it successfully.

TURN UP THE HEAT

In the practice of any exercise routine or sport, warming up the body helps prevent injuries and improve performance. Warm-up routines usually last from twenty to thirty minutes and involve all the body's major muscle groups and joints.

Strenuous physical activity leads to a buildup of lactic acid in the body, which can cause muscle aches. After activity, a twenty-minute cool-down period helps disperse lactic acid. By continuing to exercise the body but at a lesser intensity, a warm-down gradually brings down the heart rate and returns ligaments, muscles, and organs to their usual positions. Stretching eases the tension in the muscles, tendons, and ligaments. Drinking plenty of water after a training session is also important since it helps to rehydrate the body and flush out toxins.

AVOIDING TRAGEDY

The most horrifying parkour accidents have happened while performing irresponsible parkour stunts, such as roofing or roof climbing. When a traceur loses his grip high above the ground, there are no second chances. Reckless adrenaline junkies sometimes strap a GoPro camera to their heads and climb skyscrapers, bridges, and cranes as part of parkour or freerunning routines. They film themselves leaping from one roof to another high above the ground and executing handstands on narrow ledges. This is something that responsible traceurs never do. Sadly, there are many stories of people dying while performing risky and irresponsible parkour maneuvers.

GET TO THE GYM

A gym offers a controlled environment for students to learn the basics of parkour safely and under the guidance of an instructor. Participants under eighteen must first sign a waiver saying they have parental permission to practice parkour. The waiver also protects the gym from liability if a student is injured.

Members of the Urban Freeflow freerunning team are photographed during a class for teens in London. Training with a skilled coach in a gym helps minimize the risks of injury.

Since parkour is still an unregulated activity, different gyms may have different requirements for instructors. Certification programs for parkour instructors are available in person and online. The American Parkour Instructor Certification Program offers a three-day training course to experienced traceurs who wish to earn an instructor's certificate. Would-be instructors study the history and philosophy of parkour, the basics of anatomy and biomechanics relating to parkour training, the principles of exercise science, how to recognize and treat injuries, and how to successfully coach students of all ages and capabilities. They learn how to demonstrate proper form and how to correct a student's movements. At the end of the course, candidates must complete a physical and a written exam.

CHECK OUT THE COMPETITION

Some members of the parkour community believe that competitions and the corporate sponsorship associated with them are in conflict with the true spirit of parkour. Nonetheless, an avid international audience has embraced such events to practice the sport responsibly and safely. The first major competition, called Red Bull Art of Motion, was sponsored by Red Bull energy drinks and showcased freerunning techniques. That event was followed by the Barclaycard World Freerun Championships.

In the United States, the West Coast Parkour Championships hosts three events: Speed, Skill, and Freestyle. Both youth and adult athletes compete as individuals and teams.

British freerunner Ryan Doyle dazzles the crowd with a controlled twist during the Red Bull Art of Motion competition in Santorini, Greece.

Most kids have played some version of the game the Floor Is Lava. The players pretend the floor is a seething mass of hot lava, and you have to cross the room without touching the floor by climbing over the backs of couches and scrambling across tables and chairs. Some parkour competitions feature a version of this game in which traceurs must race to complete an aerial course across jungle gyms, raised platforms, and other structures, without touching the ground. This is the fun and youthful spirit of parkour.

CHAPTER FIVE

LEGENDS OF PARKOUR

In late 2018, a commercial for the latest iPhone began airing on TV. The spot, titled "Color Flood," showed hundreds of people dressed in bright coveralls streaming through an empty city, with many performing parkour moves. In just twenty-four hours, the ad generated 9.4 million likes on YouTube.

As this ad implied, parkour traditionally has focused on the community rather than on the individual "stars" of the sport. However, some traceurs have become world famous. The extreme moves these artists execute in online videos and televised competitions are the result of years of rigorous training. The following parkour and freerunning athletes have raised public awareness about this art of movement and inspired many people to join parkour gyms or begin training on their own.

SÉBASTIEN FOUCAN

Sébastien Foucan was one of the original Yamakasi, the parkour group that turned the urban environment of Lisses, France, into a large-scale obstacle course and playground.

High above Edinburgh, Scotland, former Yamakasi and extreme freerunner Sébastien Foucan shows off his artistic form and incredible physical control.

When he moved to London, Foucan began developing a style of parkour that focused on innovation, acrobatics, and creative expression. In the documentaries *Jump London* (2003) and *Jump Britain* (2005), Foucan introduced viewers to the art of movement now called freerunning. Foucan played the role of Mollaka in the 2006 James Bond film *Casino Royale*, dazzling moviegoers in a chase sequence through a construction site, with Daniel Craig (actually a stunt double) hot on his heels.

TIM SHIEFF

Tim Shieff was a breakdancer and soccer player before he discovered parkour. When he saw Sébastien Foucan executing incredible moves in *Jump Britain,* Shieff knew he'd found his calling. Since then, he has competed on *American Ninja Warrior,* a televised competition in which contestants must complete an extreme obstacle course to compete for cash prizes. The English traceur also appeared in *MTV's Ultimate Parkour Challenge*. Shieff attributes his fitness to a vegan diet, which he claims has improved the health of his joints and shortened his recovery time.

SARA MUDALLAL

Sara Mudallal has inspired Muslim women around the world to practice parkour, such as Mahsa Khakbazan, shown here during a training session at a gym in Tehran, Iran.

Sara Mudallal, who is Jordanian, started training in 2017 and became the first person to wear a hijab—the head covering worn by some Muslim women—in competition on *American Ninja Warrior*. Although there is no official uniform for parkour athletes, many people might be surprised to see someone performing these difficult moves in a hijab. Mudallal also has a black belt in karate. Along with other women practicing parkour in the Middle East, Mudallal is defying stereotypes.

VICTOR LOPEZ

Victor "Showtime" Lopez put himself on the map in 2007 when he appeared at the first Red Bull Art of Motion competition in Vienna, Austria, and scored a second-place finish. Also a stuntman, director, and photographer, Lopez cofounded the Tempest Free Running Academy in Los Angeles.

THE RUNNING OF THE BULLS

The first freerunning competition in the world, Red Bull Art of Motion, is sponsored by the maker of Red Bull energy drinks. The first two Art of Motion competitions were held in Vienna, Austria, in 2007 and 2009. The competition attracts elite freerunners from all over the world who gather in amazing locations, most recently on the island of Santorini in Greece. The event showcases a mix of freerunning, parkour, martial arts, and acrobatics, and contestants compete against a challenging course. In 2017, more than six hundred athletes from fifty-five countries had participated in Red Bull Art of Motion.

KATIE MCDONNELL

Katie McDonnell is a world-class freerunner from the United Kingdom who began as a cheerleader and dancer. Now a full-time professional freerunner, McDonnell appears in films, on television, and in advertising campaigns. She was a stunt double in the 2016 action film *Assassin's Creed* and a finalist on *Ninja Warrior UK*.

JASON PAUL

After seeing parkour in a video on the internet, Jason Paul and a friend started teaching it to themselves. After countless hours of practicing basic moves, Paul, who is German, entered a parkour competition in Trafalgar Square, London, in which he placed third. Sponsored by Red Bull

World-class parkour atheletes like Jason Paul, a regular competitor in the Art of Motion, have embraced sponsorship as a way to earn a living as they pursue their passion.

and GoPro, Paul travels around the world showing off his incredible skills.

JESSE LA FLAIR

With his signature baseball cap and more than one hundred million views of his YouTube videos, Jesse la Flair is one of the most recognizable American parkour artists. Like many talented traceurs, he has built a successful career doing stunts for movies and TV, as well as motion capture for video games. La Flair also directed and starred with Cory DeMeyers in the parkour documentary *From Here to There* (2014) and produced a web series about freerunning called *Off the Edge* in 2015.

BUILDING A BETTER TRACEUR?

In 2018, the robotics company Boston Dynamics showed off an updated version of its Atlas robot, a bipedal battery-powered machine with humanoid silver limbs and computer vision. They released a highlight reel titled "Parkour" that shows Atlas leaping over a log and jumping up a series of parkour mounts with speed and grace. Atlas can also do backflips! Many human tasks are now accomplished by robots, and some traceurs dislike the idea of a robot built to do parkour. Boston Dynamics believes that someday robots such as Atlas will be used to help rescue humans from dangerous situations.

SPANNING THE GLOBE WITH PARKOUR

From its beginnings in the suburbs of Paris, parkour has grown into a global community of practitioners who bring their own unique spin to the practice. In just a few decades, this new art of movement has made its mark on all forms of media. Parkour captures audiences around the world by proving that, with the proper training, there are no limits to what the human body can accomplish.

GLOSSARY

art of displacement An athletic activity in which the participant moves quickly and fluidly through an area by surmounting obstacles and leaping across spaces; the original name for parkour.

biomechanics The scientific study of how the human body moves and how different forces act on the body.

cat leap Leaping from one obstacle to another in a hanging and tucked position.

commercialization Managing something (like a business or a sport) entirely for profit.

discipline An activity that provides mental or physical training.

flow Smooth, consistent transitions from one skill or technique to another.

freerunning A version of parkour popularized by Sébastien Foucan that emphasizes creative expression and acrobatic moves.

jam An event where practitioners gather to do parkour together.

lactic acid An organic acid produced in the muscle tissues during a period of strenuous exercise.

liability The state of being responsible for something, especially as determined by law.

ligament A short band of elastic tissue around the joints. They connect bones or cartilage.

momentum The motion of a moving body.

mount An object that is usually under shoulder height.

obstacle course A course that participants complete by climbing over, around, pulling themselves up, vaulting over, etc., various obstacles; often used for military training.

practitioner A person who studies or engages in a discipline.

regimen A course of medical treatment, a way of life, or a diet that promotes or restores health.

tendon A cord of flexible tissue that attaches muscle to bone.

tic-tac A jumping movement from one wall to another, used to gain height.

toxin A substance that can damage the body. Toxins come from metabolic processes in organisms.

traceur A practitioner of parkour. (Traceuse is a female practitioner of parkour.)

vault To move over an obstacle by utilizing one or more hands to move the body over the obstacle.

FOR MORE INFORMATION

American Parkour Headquarters
219 M. Street NW
Washington, DC 20001
(844) 727-5687
Website: http://www.americanparkour.com
Facebook, Twitter, and YouTube: @AmericanParkour
Instagram: @americanparkour
Formed in 2002, American Parkour Headquarters runs a parkour gym in Washington, D.C., and has affiliated academies around the world. The American Parkour Headquarters website includes a Women's Community page for female practitioners.

Boise Parkour Park (Rhodes Skate Park)
1555 W Front Street
Boise, ID 83702
(208) 608-7600 (Boise Parks and Rec Administration)
Website: https://parks.cityofboise.org/parks-and-facilities/parks/rhodes-skate-park
Facebook: @Boiseparksandrecreation
Twitter: @boiseparks
Tucked under a highway overpass, this skate park near downtown Boise has plenty of fantastic structures and features for parkour.

Origins Parkour
2655 Main Street, Floor 3
Vancouver, BC
(604) 558-1779
Website: http://www.originsparkour.com
Facebook: @originsparkour

Instagram: @origins.pk
Twitter: @OriginsParkour
YouTube: Origins Parkour
As of 2019, the largest parkour gym in Canada boasts 10,000 square feet (3,048 square meters) of space, a specialized parkour park designed by athletes, a giant foam pit, and a gymnastics spring floor, among other features.

Parkour EDU
1772 Prairie Way, Unit G
Louisville, CO 80027
Email: info@parkouredu.org
Website: https://www.parkouredu.org
Facebook, Instagram, and YouTube: @parkouredu
Twitter: @ParkourEDU
The goal of this nonprofit is to empower the international parkour and freerunning community by raising awareness about training methods and promoting safe educational facilities. The site offers free content (including e-books) and parkour-related podcasts.

Parkour Visions
500 Yale Avenue
Seattle, WA 98109
(206) 923-8864
Website: https://parkourvisions.org
Facebook: @ParkourVisions
YouTube: Parkour Visions
Founded in 2007, Parkour Visions is a nonprofit organization dedicated to sharing the benefits of parkour with people of all ages through educational programming, design service, and community development support.

Penzer Action Park
4847 200 Street
Langley, British Columbia
V3A 8G2
Canada
Website: https://www.familyfuncanada.com/vancouver/penzer-action-park
Facebook: @FamilyFunVancouver
Instagram: @familyfuncanada
Twitter: @familyfunyvr
Completed in 2017, this park is the largest outdoor parkour facility in Canada. The park has a parkour area designed for children four and under and full-size features for older kids and adults.

World Freerunning Parkour Federation
602 Industrial Court
Hartland, WI 53029
Email: contact@wfpf.com
Website: https://wfpf.com
Facebook and Twitter: @worldfpf
Instagram: @thewfpf
YouTube: World Freerunning Parkour Federation
This worldwide organization of athletes is dedicated to bringing the sport and philosophy of parkour to mainstream audiences everywhere.

FOR FURTHER READING

Boyer, Jeff. *A Beginner's Guide to Parkour: Discover the Freedom and Excitement of Free Running.* Seattle, WA: CreateSpace Publishing, 2014.

Butler, Erin K. *Extreme Land Sports* (Sports to the Extreme). Mankato, MN: Capstone Press, 2017.

Ford, Ryan, and Ben Musholt. *Parkour Strength Training: Overcome Obstacles for Fun and Fitness*. Seattle, WA: CreateSpace Publishing, 2016.

Fury, Sam. *Essential Parkour Training: Basic Parkour Strength and Movement*. Seattle, WA: CreateSpace Publishing, 2017.

Greek, Joe. *Parkour*. (Sports to the Extreme). New York, NY: Rosen, 2015.

Henry, Max. *Parkour Roadmap.* Herndon, VA: Mascot Books, 2017.

Howard, J. J. *Tracers*. New York, NY: G. P. Putnam's Sons, 2015.

Hulse, Julian. *Free Running: The Ultimate Guide for Understanding Parkour and What You Must Know About It.* Seattle, WA: CreateSpace Publishing, 2014.

Jackson, Demi. *Parkour*. New York, NY: Gareth Stevens Publishing, 2015.

Killcoyne, Hope Lourie, ed. *Extreme Sports and Its Greatest Competitors.* New York, NY: Rosen, 2015.

Mason Crest Publishers. *Extreme Sports* (Inside the World of Sports Series). Broomall, PA: Mason Crest Publishers, 2017.

BIBLIOGRAPHY

American Parkour. "APK Instructor Certification Program." Retrieved January 23, 2019. http://americanparkour.com/academy/parkour-instructor-certification.

Ana. "Red Bull 'Art of Motion' Freerunning and Parkour Competition in Santorini." *The National Herald*, October 8, 2017. https://www.thenationalherald.com/177515/red-bull-art-motion-freerunning-parkour-competition-santorini.

Brazier, Brendan. "Moving on up with the vegan prince of parkour." Alive.com, January 25, 2017. https://www.alive.com/lifestyle/moving-on-up-tim-shieff.

Edwardes, Dan. *The Parkour and Freerunning Handbook.* New York, NY: HarperCollins, 2009.

Ferguson, Dan. "Video: Largest Outdoor Parkour Park in Canada Opens in Langley City Thursday, June 29." *Surrey-Now Leader*, June 26, 2017. https://www.surreynowleader.com/news/video-largest-outdoor-parkour-park-in-canada-opens-in-langley-city-thursday-june-29.

Glader, Paul. "Inside the Creative Battle to Lead the Core of Parkour." *Forbes,* November 25, 2017. https://www.forbes.com.

Hale, James Loke. "Creators Going Pro: Parkour Team STORROR Has Built Up a YouTube Business to Dizzying Heights, Aims Higher with New Venture." Tubefilter.com, January 16, 2019. https://www.tubefilter.com/2019/01/16/creators-going-pro-storror.

Lawler, Richard. "Boston Dynamics' Atlas robot shows upgraded ability in 'Parkour' video." Engadget.com, October 11, 2018. https://www.engadget.com/2018/10/11/atlas-robot-parkour-boston-dynamics.

Lawrence, Cameron. "How Parkour Works." Howstuffworks, May 2, 2006. https://adventure.howstuffworks.com/outdoor-activities/urban-sports/parkour1.htm.

Limitless Pursuits. "Jason Paul: freerunning from Trafalgar Square to the skyscrapers of Bangkok." Limitlesspursuits.com, July 28, 2018. https://limitlesspursuits.com.

Musholt, Ben. "Parkour Injury Survey Summary." December 20, 2016. https://www.benmusholt.com/parkour/parkour-injury-rates-2016.

Pierce, Chad. M. "Is Parkour Illegal? The Legal Situation in the U.S." Ultimate Parkour Gear, June 20, 2018. https://ultimateparkourgear.com/is-parkour-illegal.

Press Association. "UK becomes first country to recognise parkour as a sport." *The Guardian*, January 10, 2017. https://www.theguardian.com/sport/2017/jan/10/uk-first-country-recognise-parkour-sport.

Red Bull. "Meet Sara Mudallel, a parkour athlete." Redbull.com, September 26, 2018. https://www.redbull.com/mea-en/meet-sara-mudallal-a-parkour-athlete.

Toorock, Mark. "One Year in, D.C. Public Schools Parkour Program Has Kids Leaping with Confidence." American Parkour, February 12, 2018. http://americanparkour.com/news/dc-public-schools-one-year-after-parkour-is-introduced.

Toorock, Mark. "Sébastien Foucan: A life in movement." American Parkour, April 23, 2018. http://americanparkour.com/news/sebastien-foucan-a-life-in-movement.

University of Southampton. "From Maths Graduate to Ninja Warrior." February 20, 2018. https://connects.soton.ac.uk/feature/from-maths-graduate-to-ninja-warrior.

Witfeld, Jan, Ilona E. Gerling, and Alexander Pach. *The Ultimate Parkour & Freerunning Book.* Maidenhead, UK: Meyer and Meyer Sport (UK), Ltd., 2010.

World Freerunning Parkour Federation. "What Is Parkour?" Retrieved January 24, 2019. https://wfpf.com/parkour.

Zwadlo, Chad. "Safety in Parkour." American Parkour, December 8, 2013. http://americanparkour.com/articles/safety-in-parkour-chad-zwadlo.

INDEX

ABOUT THE AUTHOR

Monique Vescia is the author of dozens of nonfiction books on a variety of subjects, including *Extreme Sports and Stunts: Trampoline*. She lives in Seattle, home of the parkour hotspot Freeway Park. Her teenage son spent many hours training with his friends at a parkour gym in their neighborhood.

PHOTO CREDITS

Cover, p. 1 Tempura/E+/Getty Images; p. 5 Taras-studio/Shutterstock.com; p. 7 © Excelsior–L'Equipe/Roger-Viollet/The Image Works; p. 9 © AP Images; p. 10 Tara Walton/Toronto Star/Getty Images; p. 14 Rommel Canlas/Shutterstock.com; p. 16 Kaliam/Shutterstock.com; p. 19 Gareth Brown/Corbis/Getty Images; p. 21 Agencja Fotograficzna Caro/Alamy Stock Photo; p. 24 wundervisuals/E+/Getty Images; p. 25 Mint Images/Getty Images; p. 28 Leon Neal/AFP/Getty Images; pp. 30, 35 Vladimir Rys Photography/Getty Images; p. 32 PYMCA/Universal Images Group/Getty Images; p. 33 Behrouz Mehri/AFP/Getty Images; cover and interior graphic elements AdrianHillman/iStock/Getty Images (parkour silhouette); RDC_design/iStock/Getty Images (orange grunge background); Vijay Patel/DigitalVision Vectors/Getty Images (black dots background).

Design and Layout: Michael Moy; Photo Researcher: Sherri Jackson